LOGIC AND PSYCHOLOGY

LOGIC AND PSYCHOLOGY

BY

JEAN PIAGET

With an Introduction
on Piaget's Logic by

W. MAYS

BASIC BOOKS, INC.
Publishers, New York

B
—
B
First Printing, 1957
Second Printing, 1958
Published in the United States
by Basic Books, Inc., by arrangement with
Manchester University Press
Library of Congress Catalog Card Number: 57-10774

PREFACE

THIS BOOK is based on three lectures which were given in the University of Manchester in October 1952. I should like to thank Professor Polanyi for arranging these lectures, Dr. Mays and Dr. Whitehead who translated them, and the members of the University of Manchester who formed my audience. In Manchester, where the name of Jevons is still remembered, this attempt to relate logic to psychology met with a particularly encouraging response.

1953   JEAN PIAGET

CONTENTS

AN ELEMENTARY INTRODUCTION TO PIAGET'S LOGIC

By W. Mays

FROM ABOUT 1939 onwards Piaget has, at Geneva, been applying the techniques of symbolic logic to the study of the intellectual behaviour of the child in an attempt to obtain some insight into the way in which the child's logical, mathematical and physical concepts arise. In his *Traité de logique* (Colin, 1949) he has outlined systematically the logical principles used in these investigations. And since the logical treatment of this book is largely based upon the above work, a short introductory survey is given of some of its more important concepts.

This account falls under five headings. In (1) the elements of symbolic logic are briefly dealt with together with the concept of a logical calculus; (2) deals with the class interpretation of this calculus and with classificatory systems; (3) with the propositional interpretation and the logical relations holding between any two propositions. In (4) some account is given of the nature of a mathematical group, since the system of propositions resembles such a group, whilst (5) deals with lattices, since Boolean algebra, upon which modern logic is based, is in its mathematical treatment subsumed under lattice theory.

It is Piaget's claim that psychologists have in symbolic logic an instrument as useful as statistics. Symbolic logic has already been applied to diverse fields—to language, to the design of logical and mathematical computers, to biology, and nerve-networks. Piaget has shown how it may be fruitfully applied to the analysis of the intellectual activities of the child.

*   *   *

1. *Elements*

In symbolic logic we make use of variables similar to those used in algebra (i.e. x, y, z), but instead of referring to numbers, they refer in the propositional calculus solely to propositions, e.g. 'The sun is shining', 'Mary is singing'. We represent them by the letters p, q, r, s, etc. Just as we use such operations as $+, -, \times, \div$ in algebra, so in symbolic logic we use similar signs to refer to relations between propositions.

They are

      (1) not (negation) $-$

      (2) and (conjunction) $\cdot$

      (3) or (disjunction (either or both))   v

      (4) if . . . then (implication)   ⊃

Any logical operation can be expressed in terms of either $\cdot$ and negation or v and negation.

From this we can build up other relations such as equivalence $= (p=q)$ or incompatibility $/ (p/q)$, e.g.: 'It is not the case both that it is raining (p) and the pavement is dry (q).' Further, there is a resemblance between the $+$ and $\times$ of ordinary algebra and the v and $\cdot$ operations of symbolic logic. This identification was first made by George Boole in his algebra of logic; pvq and $p{\cdot}q$ are therefore sometimes called the logical sum and logical product and the operations v and $\cdot$ logical addition and logical multiplication. Boolean algebra is really an algebra of 1 and 0, since in this system propositions can only have two values: truth and falsity.

2. *Classes*

The abstract algebra of logic can be given a number of interpretations. The propositional and class interpretations are alone considered here. In the class-calculus we start with the concept of a class of objects. A class may be defined as all those entities having a certain property; for example, the class of all men, or the class of all tigers. We may start with a class C, and denote sub-classes of C by A, B. Thus C might be a square and A, B, the sub-classes of points in different regions of C (Fig. 1). In mathematics the concept of a class is referred to as a *set*.

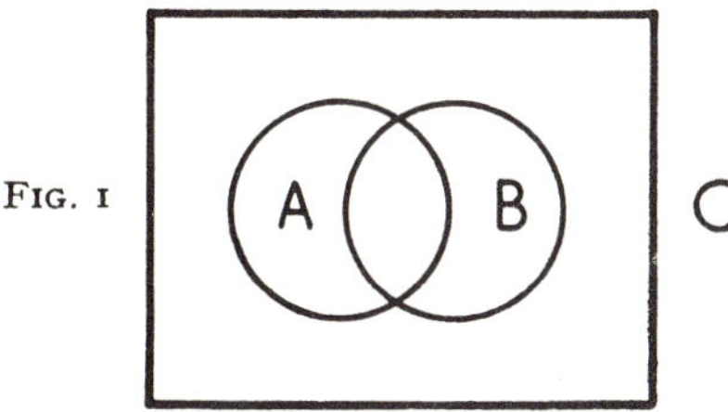

Fig. 1

Similar relations hold between classes as between propositions, but to avoid confusion different symbols are used. Piaget uses the arithmetical sum and product signs $+, \times$.

The division of a class C may also be depicted as follows:

Table (*a*)   Example:

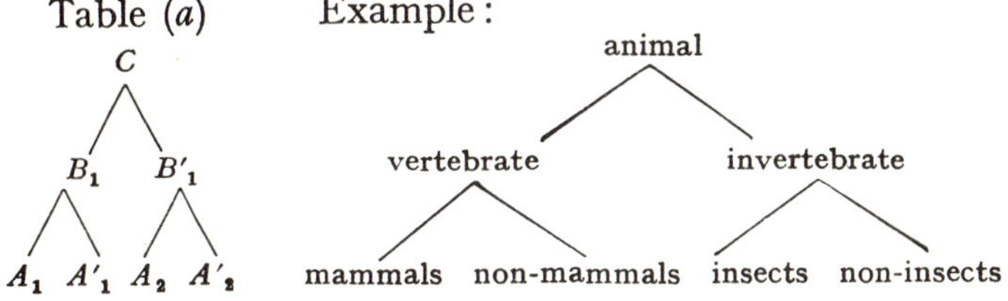

Consider another method of classification. Suppose B_1 and B_2 are two distinct classes, such that all the individuals of B_1 are part of B_2 and reciprocally.

Let B_1 be animals, A_1 vertebrates, A'_1 invertebrates. Let B_2 be the distribution of animals according to their habitat, A_2 terrestrial and A'_2 aquatic. We thus get four different combinations:

Table (*b*)

$A_1 A_2$	$A'_1 A_2$
$A_1 A'_2$	$A'_1 A'_2$

vertebrates terrestrial (A_1A_2)
vertebrates aquatic $(A_1A'_2)$
invertebrates terrestrial (A'_1A_2)
invertebrates aquatic $(A'_1A'_2)$.

The multiplication of $B_1 \times B_2$ therefore gives us animals distributed according as to whether they live on land or in the sea and have the characteristic of being either vertebrate or invertebrate. As Piaget expresses it

$$B_1 \times B_2 = A_1A_2 + A_1A'_2 + A'_1A_2 + A'_1A'_2.$$

Type (*a*) classifications in terms of dichotomous divisions are found in botanical and zoological classifications. Piaget has such systems in mind when he speaks of additive groupements of classes.

Type (*b*) two-way classificatory systems, expressing qualitative correspondences, are used as above in zoology. Such systems form Piaget's multiplicative groupements of classes.

3. *Propositions*

In the case of (*b*), Piaget points out that there is a correspondence between the multiplication of classes and the conjunction of propositions, since of any two propositions p and q each can be either true or false.

Combining these two at a time, we obtain

$$p \cdot q \ \text{v} \ p \cdot \bar{q} \ \text{v} \ \bar{p} \cdot q \ \text{v} \ \bar{p} \cdot \bar{q},$$

which may be read off from the following diagram:

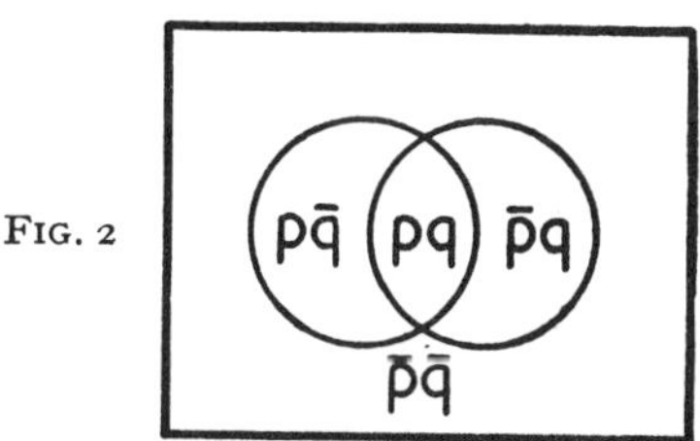

Fig. 2

As each of these pairs may itself be either true or false, we obtain sixteen possible arrangements. Each type of relation between propositions may be translated in terms of one of these arrangements.

Examples: $p \text{v} q = p \cdot q \ \text{v} \ p \cdot \bar{q} \ \text{v} \ \bar{p} \cdot q$ [$\bar{p} \cdot \bar{q}$ is false]
$p \cdot q = p \cdot q$ [$p \cdot \bar{q} \ \text{v} \ \bar{p} \cdot q \ \text{v} \ \bar{p} \cdot \bar{q}$ are false]
$p \supset q = p \cdot q \ \text{v} \ \bar{p} \cdot q \ \text{v} \ \bar{p} \cdot \bar{q}$ [$p \cdot \bar{q}$ is false].

The pairs which are false are shaded in the resultant diagrams, thus we have

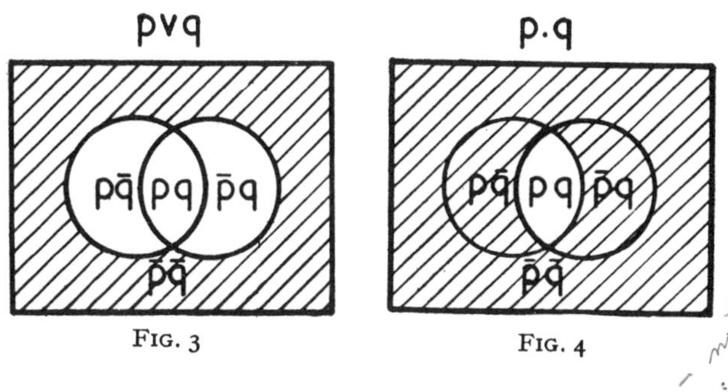

Fig. 3   Fig. 4

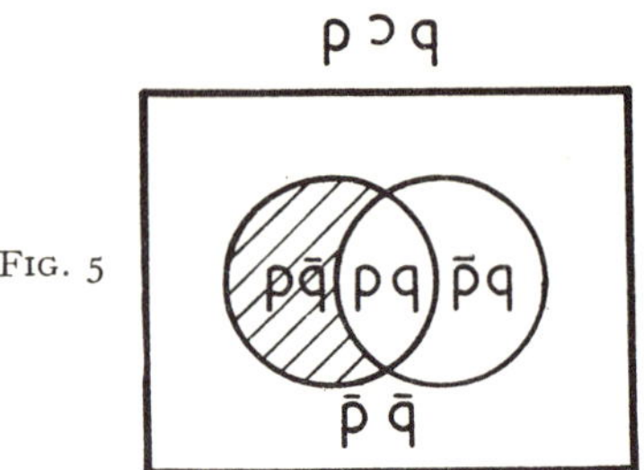

FIG. 5

Piaget states that every such relationship has an inverse (complementary), a reciprocal and a correlate.

1. Inverse (N). If, e.g., the proposition is pvq it has for its complementary $\bar{p}\cdot\bar{q}$ (if we negate $\bar{p}\cdot\bar{q}$ thus $\overline{\bar{p}\cdot\bar{q}}$ we arrive back at pvq).

2. Reciprocal (R) of pvq is the same proposition but with negation signs added, i.e. $\bar{p}$v$\bar{q}$.

3. Correlate (C) is the proposition obtained when we substitute a v whenever a · occurs, and vice versa. Thus $p\cdot q$ becomes pvq, and pvq becomes $p\cdot q$.

4. Identity operator (I) is the operation which, when performed on any proposition, leaves it unchanged.

The following table (c), *Traité de logique*, p. 271, shows how the first three operations are related

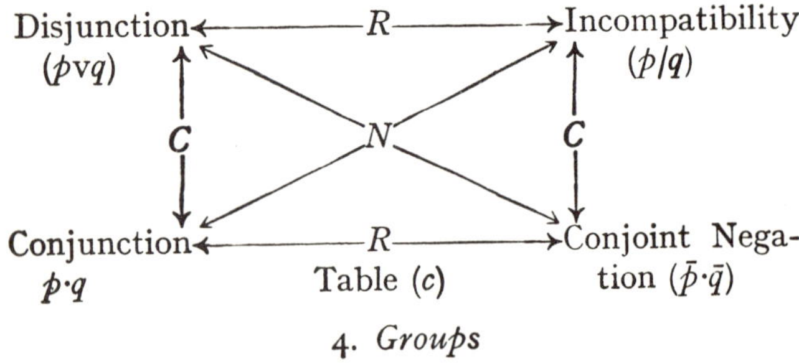

4. *Groups*

The above set of transformations N, R, C together with I constitute an abstract group. One example of a group (*Traité de logique*, p. 92) is the system of positive and negative numbers characterized by the operation $+n$ (addition of an integer).

It obeys the four conditions.

1. Two operations of the system have for their resultant a new operation of the system $+1+1=2$.

2. Every operation of the system can be annulled by an inverse operation $+2-2=0$.

3. There exists one, and only one, identity operator (o) which is the resultant of every operation and its inverse, and such that when applied to any operation it does not change it:

$$| \; 1 - 1 - 0 \text{ and } 1 \pm 0 = 1.$$

4. The operations are associative $(4+2)-3=4+(2-3)$.

5. *Lattices*

Boolean algebra may be considered as a special case of certain abstract mathematical systems called lattices. A lattice has certain limiting conditions—*join* and *meet*. In the case of any two classes X and Y, the *join* is the smallest of the classes in which X and Y are both included, and the *meet* is the largest class included both in X and in Y.

The following classificatory system (Table (d)), given by Piaget in his *Traité de logique*, p. 95, can be considered as a semi-lattice. A branch leading from one element to another means that the latter is included in it.

Table (d)

Each pair of classes possesses a *join*, B for A and A', C for A and B', or C for A' and B', etc., since it is the smallest class which includes both. As for the *meet*, A is the *meet* of A and of B, or of A and of C, etc., since it is the largest class included in both. On the other hand, the *meet* of two disjunctive classes is null, which is, of course, the definition of disjunction (i.e. they are excluded from each other), e.g. A and A', A and B', A' and B' all $=0$.

AUTHOR'S INTRODUCTION

THE AIM of this book is not to discover how psychological theories may be formalized by means of logic,* but to study the application of logical techniques to the psychological facts themselves, and especially to the thought structures found at different levels of intellectual development.

This problem is of both theoretical and practical interest.

Theoretically, it is important to ask what sort of correspondence exists between the structures described by logic and the actual thought processes studied by psychology. The question whether the structures and operations of logic correspond to anything in our actual thought, and whether the latter conforms to logical laws, is still an open one.

Practically, it is important to discover in what way logic can advance psychological research. In our opinion its chief value does not lie in axiomatizing psychological theories; a great gap still exists between the relative imprecision of such theories and the deductive rigour of logical systems. On the other hand, the algebra of logic can help us to specify psychological structures, and to put into calculus form those operations and structures central to our actual thought processes. Psychologists have no hesitation in using mathematics for calculating correlation coefficients, for factor analysis, etc. Now the algebra of logic is

---

* F. B. Fitch and C. L. Hull are among the best known of those who have attempted such a formalization.

a sub-system of one of the most general fields of mathematics, that of 'abstract algebra'. The fact that it is concerned with qualitative structures in no way detracts from its mathematical character; modern mathematicians are coming more and more to emphasize the importance of such structures. The psychologist for his part welcomes the qualitative character of logic, since it facilitates the analysis of the actual structures underlying intellectual operations, as contrasted with the quantitative treatment of their behavioural outcome. Most 'tests' of intelligence measure the latter, but our real problem is to discover the actual operational mechanisms which govern such behaviour, and not simply to measure it. The algebra of logic can therefore help the psychologist, by giving him a precise method of specifying the structures which emerge in the analysis of the operational mechanisms of thought.

To give a concrete example to which reference will be made again: psychologists have shown that at the age of 12 the child is able to discover elementary combinatorial operations (combinations 2 by 2, 3 by 3, or 4 by 4 in the random drawing of coloured counters, etc., from a bag).* This the child discovers without, of course, being aware of the mathematical formulae involved, by finding a systematic method of completing the combinations at the same level of intellectual development at which he begins to use propositional operations (such as $p \supset q$, i.e. 'if then', or $p \lor q$, p/q, etc.). We may then enquire why these two kinds of operations, which at first sight seem quite unrelated, nevertheless appear simultaneously in the child's

---

* See Piaget and Inhelder, *La Genèse de l'idée de hasard chez l'enfant*, Paris, 1951 (Presses Universitaires de France), chap. vii.

behaviour. The algebra of logic makes it immediately clear that propositional operations are based upon a combinatorial system not involved, for example, in the elementary structures of classes and relations which children aged 7 to 12, on the average, use. By submitting the operational structures to logical analysis, we can thus easily explain why such varied types of behaviour occur simultaneously. In this way, the algebra of logic can constantly aid the psychologist in his studies.

However, at the present time there is little collaboration between logicians and psychologists. Indeed, there is a mutual distrust which makes cooperation difficult. A brief historical survey will explain how this has come about.

I

HISTORY AND STATUS OF
THE PROBLEM

IN THE nineteenth century before Boole, de Morgan, Jevons, etc., developed the algebra of logic, and before experimental psychology became a science, no such conflict between logic and psychology existed. Classical logic believed it was possible to discover the actual structure of thought processes, and the general structures underlying the external world as well as the normative laws of the mind. Classical philosophical psychology, in its turn, considered the laws of logic and the laws of ethics to be implicit in the mental functioning of each normal individual. These two disciplines then at no point had grounds for disagreement.

But with the development of the young science of experimental psychology logical factors were excluded; intelligence was explained by sensations, images, associations and other mechanisms. The reaction to this approach was unfortunate; for example, certain members of the Würzburg school of *Denkpsychologie* introduced logical relations to complete the action of psychological factors in judgment.

Logic was thus used in the causal explanation of the psychological facts themselves. To this fallacious use of logic in psychology the name of 'logicism' has been given, and, if psychologists generally are distrustful of logic, it is due mainly to their fear of falling into this fallacy. Most present-day psychologists try to explain intelligence without any appeal to logical theory.

At about the time that psychologists were trying to divorce their science from logic, the founders of modern logic or 'logistic' asked for it to be separated from psychology for similar reasons. It is true that Boole, the inventor of the algebra that bears his name, still believed he was describing 'The Laws of Thought', but this was because he held these to be essentially algebraic in nature. With an increase in the deductive rigour and formal character of logical systems, one of the chief tasks of the later logicians has been to eliminate from the field of logic any appeal to intuition, that is to say, to any kind of psychological factor. When there is recourse to such factors in logic the fallacy is called 'psychologism'. This term has been used by logicians to refer to insufficiently formalized logical theories, just as psychologists have used the term 'logicism' to refer to psychological theories insufficiently tested by experience.

Most logicians today are no longer concerned with whether the laws and structures of logic bear any sort of relation to psychological structures. A French disciple of Bertrand Russell, at the turn of this century, even asserted that the concept of an 'operation' was essentially anthropomorphic, and that logical operations were, in fact, only formal operations having no resemblance whatever to psychological operations. As logic has perfected its formal rigour, logicians have ceased to interest themselves in the study of actual thought processes. Bernays held, for example, and from the standpoint of a perfectly formalized axiomatic logic he is undoubtedly right, that logical relations are strictly applicable only to mathematical deduction, since every other form of thought merely has an approximate character.

When we try to discover the entities to which these logical structures correspond, we find that the progressive formalization of logic has given rise to four possible solutions, which must be briefly examined from the point of view of their bearing on psychology.

First, there is *platonism*, which was a feature of the early work of Bertrand Russell and A. N. Whitehead, which stimulated the work of Scholz, and which remains either the confessed or unconfessed ideal of a large number of logicians. Logic on such a view corresponds to a system of universals existing independently of experience and non-psychological in origin. However, we still have to explain how the mind comes to discover such universals. The platonic hypothesis only shelves this problem and brings us no nearer a solution.

The second solution is *conventionalism*, which holds that logical entities owe their existence and laws to a system of conventions, or generally accepted rules. But this leaves us with the problem of why these conventions should be so successful, and so surprisingly effective in their application.

The notion of convention has therefore given place to that of a *well-formed language*. This third solution, put forward by the Vienna Circle, has strongly influenced logical empiricism. It distinguishes empirical truths, or non-tautological relationships, and tautologies or purely syntactical relationships, which, with the aid of an appropriate semantics, may be used to express empirical truths. We have here, for the first time, a theory having psychological significance which may be tested empirically. Psychologically, however, it entails several difficulties.

In the first place, we cannot speak about pure experience or 'empirical truths' apart from logical relationships. In other words, experience cannot be interpreted in abstraction from the conceptual and logical apparatus which makes such an interpretation possible. In our experiments with Mlle Inhelder,* in which young children were asked to say whether the surface of the water in inclined glass tubes was horizontal or not, we found that children do not perceive 'horizontality' before they are able to construct a spatial framework of reference. Now, in order to construct such a framework, they require geometrical operations, and in the construction of such operations logical operations have to be used.

Secondly, logical relationships throughout the whole period of their development never appear as a simple system of linguistic or symbolic expressions but always imply a group of operations.†

For example, children from 5 to 8 years of age are shown an open box in which there are twenty wooden beads (the class formed by the whole twenty will be called B). Most of the beads are brown (forming a class A) but some are white (class A': therefore $B=A+A'$). The child is asked the simple question: 'Are there more brown beads (A) in this box or more wooden beads (B)?' A disciple of the Vienna Circle would reply that we have here a simple empirical fact of which even the youngest child can take note, and which is based on the propositions 'all the beads are

* Piaget and Inhelder, *La Représentation de l'espace chez l'enfant*, Paris (P.U.F.).

† This also remains true when the subjects have arrived at maturity.

made of wood, but they are not all brown' (as a matter of fact the child immediately agrees with these two assertions). We have also a system of logical relationships by means of which this 'empirical truth' may be expressed in terms of a precise symbolism, giving us in this case a simple inclusion between two classes, $A < B$, i.e. 'the part A is smaller than the whole B'.

Now psychological experiments definitely show that the child between 5 and 7 years is unable to construct this inclusion $A < B$. His own interpretation of the facts leads him to conclude (and once again this demonstrates that the interpretation of perceptual data presupposes a previous logical elaboration) that $A > B$ because $A > A'$. His answer is: 'There are more brown beads (A) than wooden beads (B) because there are only two or three white ones (A')'. What this answer really means is: either the question deals with the whole class (B), and then all the beads are wooden ones, or it deals with a part (A); but if the whole is split up into its constituent parts we no longer have a whole. In this case it is reduced to the other part (A'), hence $A > B$ because $B = A'$. In other words, children find it difficult to reason about the whole and the parts at the same time. If they think of the whole, they forget the parts and vice versa.* In order to construct the inclusion $A < B$, which, on the average, can be done between the ages of 7 and 8 years, the child has not simply to carry out a verbal or symbolic translation of the perceptual data, but an operational composition or decomposition † of its elements: $B = A + A'$, hence

* See Piaget, *The Child's Conception of Number* (Routledge & Kegan Paul), chap. vii.

† Translator's note: In the mathematical theory of sets, the operation of composition refers to that operation which, when applied to, say, two elements A, A', produces a new set B. Con-

$A = B - A'$ and $A' = B - A$, hence $A < B$. The logical relationship is, consequently, much more than a linguistic expression which translates the empirical properties of objects. It is the resultant of the *reversible actions of composition and decomposition*, which consist of actual operations of grouping or regrouping carried out on objects.

A third difficulty prevents us from accepting the thesis that logic is merely a language. If this hypothesis were valid, logic ought to be an essential feature of the child's intellectual make-up. We would expect, on the one hand, a simple interpretation of the perceptual facts, and, on the other, a simple verbal translation of these facts as basic as language itself. But if perceptions presuppose a preliminary conceptual interpretation involving logical relationships, and if these relationships presuppose actions and organized operations, there is an interaction between perceptions and operations which ought to take a lengthy period of time to establish itself. And, in fact, logic appears relatively late in the thinking of children: the first operations dealing with classes occur between 7 and 8, on the average, and those concerned with propositions between 11 and 12. From 8 to 9, for example, the child will state that a brass bar A weighs the same as another bar B, and that as the latter weighs the same as a lead ball C, $A = B$ and $B = C$. But he rejects the conclusion that $A = C$ since from past experience he expects the relation $A < C$, and says 'B certainly weighs as much as the ball C, but with A it will be different!' Transitivity is

---

versely, the operation of decomposition refers to that operation which, when applied to the set B, splits it up into its constituent elements A, A'.

therefore still absent from the picture (i.e. there is no duplication of a formal pattern), and this state of affairs continues as long as the weight relationships remain unstructured by a preliminary group of operations (seriation, etc.).

This brings us to the fourth and last of the ways of interpreting logical relationships; *operationalism*. Championed at first by Bridgman in the United States, it has today a following in many countries (cf. the Italian operationalist movement, of which Ceccato and others are members). Unlike the preceding interpretations, operationalism provides real ground on which logic and psychology can meet. Operations (in spite of Couturat!) play an indispensable rôle in logic, since logic is based on an abstract algebra and made up of symbolic manipulations. On the other hand, operations are actual psychological activities, and all effective knowledge is based on such a system of operations.

In order to determine the relations between logic and psychology we need, therefore, (1) to construct a psychological theory of operations in terms of their genesis and structure; (2) to examine logical operations, treating them as algebraic calculi and as *structured wholes*;* and (3) to compare the results of these two kinds of enquiries.

* Translator's note: By a *structured whole*,'structure d'ensemble', Piaget refers to a system of elements defined by a general set of laws, such as the laws which define a group or a lattice. For example, a logical groupement (see pp. 26-8) is defined by a set of five operations, and in this sense forms a 'structure d'ensemble' (since the laws define the system as a whole) and is thus to be distinguished from the individual operations themselves.

II

PSYCHOLOGICAL DEVELOPMENT
OF OPERATIONS

PSYCHOLOGICALLY, operations are actions which are internalizable, reversible, and coordinated into systems characterized by laws which apply to the system as a whole. They are actions, since they are carried out on objects before being performed on symbols. They are internalizable, since they can also be carried out in thought without losing their original character of actions. They are reversible as against simple actions which are irreversible. In this way, the operation of combining can be inverted immediately into the operation of dissociating, whereas the act of writing from left to right cannot be inverted to one of writing from right to left without a new habit being acquired differing from the first. Finally, since operations do not exist in isolation they are connected in the form of *structured wholes*. Thus, the construction of a class implies a classificatory system and the construction of an asymmetrical transitive relation, a system of serial relations, etc. The construction of the number system similarly presupposes an understanding of the numerical succession: $n+\mathit{1}$.

From the point of view of psychology, the criterion for the appearance of such operational systems is the construction of invariants or concepts of conservation. In the case (see pp. 4-6) of the inclusion $A < B$ of brown beads in the larger class of wooden beads, the appearance of the operations $A+A'=B$ and $A=B-A'$ is marked by the conservation of the whole B. Before the stage at which operations are formed, however, B is destroyed as soon as it is divided into its parts A and A'. Conservation has thus to be conceived as the resultant of operational reversibility.

There are four main stages in the construction of operations, and these extend over the period from birth to maturity.

(1) *The sensori-motor period (0 to 2 years).* Before language appears the small child can only perform motor actions, without thought activity, but such actions display some of the features of intelligence, as we normally understand it; for example, the child will draw a coverlet towards itself, so as to obtain an object placed on it.

Sensori-motor intelligence is not, however, operational in character, as the child's actions have not yet been internalized in the form of representations (thought). But in practice even this type of intelligence shows a certain tendency towards reversibility, which is already evidence of the construction of certain invariants.

The most important of these invariants is that involved in the construction of the permanent object. An object can be said to attain a permanent character when it is recognized as continuing to exist beyond the limits of the perceptual field, when it is no longer felt, seen, or heard, etc. At first, objects are never thought of as permanent; the infant gives up any attempt to find them as soon as they are hidden behind or under a screen. For example, when a watch is covered with a handkerchief the child, instead of lifting the handkerchief, withdraws his hand. When the child begins to look behind the screen, he does not at first note the object's successive changes of position. If, for example, it was at A when he rediscovered it, he will continue to look for it at A after it has been moved to B, etc. Only towards the end of the first year does the object become permanent in its surrounding spatial field.*

The object's permanent character results from the organization of the spatial field, which is brought about by the coordination of the child's movements. These coordinations presuppose that the child is able to return to his starting-point (reversibility), and to change the direction of his movements (associativity), and hence they tend to take on the form of a 'group'. The construction of this first invariant is thus a resultant of reversibility in its initial phase. Sensori-motor space, in its development, attains an equilibrium by becoming organized by such a 'group of displacements', from which H. Poincaré assumed it originated, but which, in fact, is its final form of equilibrium.† The permanent object is then an invariant constructed by means of such a group; and thus even at the sensori-motor stage one observes the dual tendency of intelligence towards reversibility and conservation.

(2) *Pre-operational thought (2 to 7 years).* Towards $1\frac{1}{2}$ to 2 years the 'symbolic function' appears: language, symbolic play (the beginning of fictional invention), deferred imitation, i.e. occurring some time after the original event, and that kind of internalized imitation which gives rise to mental imagery. As a result of the

* See Piaget, *La Construction du réel chez l'enfant* (Delachaux et Niestlé), chap. i.   † *Ibid.* chap. ii.

symbolic function, 'representation formation', that is to say, the internalization of actions into thoughts, becomes possible. The field in which intelligence plays a part becomes considerably enlarged. To actions occurring in the child's immediate spatial environment, are added actions occurring in the past (as engendered by story-telling), and elsewhere, e.g. in distant space, as well as the mental division of objects and collections into parts, etc. The practical reversibility of the sensori-motor period no longer suffices for the solution of all problems, as most of them now require the intervention of definite psychological operations.

However, the child cannot immediately construct such operations; several years of preparation and organization are still required. In fact, it is much more difficult to reproduce an action correctly in thought than to carry it out on the behavioural level. The child of 2 years, for example, is able to coordinate his movements from place to place (when he walks about the room or in the garden) into a group, as well as his movements when he turns objects round. But a lengthy period of time will elapse before he will be able to represent them precisely in thought; in reproducing, for example, from memory with the help of objects, a plan of the room or garden, or in inverting the positions of objects in thought by turning the plan round.

Throughout the period from 2 to 7 years, on the average, there is an absence of reversible operations, and an absence of concepts of conservation on any level higher than the sensori-motor. For example, when the child aged 4 to 6 pours liquid or beads from one glass bottle into another of a different shape, he still believes that the actual quantity in the recipient bottle is increased or diminished in the process. He believes two sticks of equal length are equal if their end-points coincide; but if we push one of them a little way in front of the other, he thinks that the stick has been lengthened. And he believes the distance between two objects changes if a third object is put between them. When equal parts are taken away from two equal whole figures, he refuses to believe that the remainders are equal if the perceptual configurations are different.* In all fields which involve continuous or discrete quantities, one comes across the same phenomenon: when the most elementary forms of conservation are absent, it is a consequence of the absence of operational reversibility. This becomes immediately apparent as soon as there is a conflict between the perceptual configuration and logic. The child's judgments of quantity thus lack systematic transitivity. If given two quantities A and B, and then afterwards two quantities B and C, each pair can be recognized as equal ($A = B$ and $B = C$) without the first quantity A being judged equal to the last C.

We once regarded this period as 'pre-logical'. Mrs. Isaacs, Miss Hazlett and many others rightly criticized this view, since some of the early evidence which we thought satisfactory was too verbal in character. Starting from the postulate that all logical problems arise in the first place from manipulations of objects, we can now say that this period is pre-operational. Our position is then identical with theirs, if we consider logic as being based essentially on operations;

* For a fuller account see Piaget, *The Child's Conception of Number* (Routledge), and Piaget, Inhelder and Szeminska, *La Géométrie spontanée de. l'enfant*, Paris (P.U.F.).

but with the proviso that the first operations only appear between 7 and 8 years, on the average, and in a concrete form (i.e. they are carried out on objects), whilst verbal or propositional operations only arise towards 11 and 12.

(3) *Concrete operations (7 to 11 years)*. The various types of thought activity which arise during the preceding period, finally attain a state of 'mobile' equilibrium, that is to say, they acquire the character of reversibility (of being able to return to their original state or starting-point). In this way, logical operations result from the coordination of the actions of combining, dissociating, ordering and the setting up of correspondences, which then acquire the form of reversible systems.

We are still dealing only with operations carried out on the objects themselves. These concrete operations belong to the logic of classes and relations, but do not take into account the totality of possible transformations of classes and relations (i.e. their combinatorial possibilities). A careful analysis of such operations is therefore necessary, so as to bring out their limitations as well as their positive features.

One of the first important operational systems is that of *classification* or the inclusion of classes under each other: for example, sparrows $(A)<$ birds $(B)<$ animals $(C)<$ living beings (D); or we may take any other similar system of class-inclusions. Such a system (cf. p. 27) permits the following operations:

$A + A' = B$; $B + B' = C$; etc. (where $A \times A' = 0$; $B \times B' = 0$, etc.)

$B - A' = A$; $C - B' = B$; etc.

We have seen why these operations are necessary for the construction of the relation of inclusion.

A second equally important operational system is that of *seriation*, or the linking of asymmetrical transitive relations into a system. For example, the child is given a certain number of unequal rods $A, B, C, D \ldots$ to arrange in order of increasing length. If the rods are markedly unequal, there is no logical problem and he can construct a series by relying on observation alone. But if the variation in length is small, so that the rods have to be compared two at a time before they can be arranged in such a series, the following is observed. Before the age of 7, on the average, the child proceeds unsystematically by comparing the pairs BD, AE, CG, etc., and then corrects the results. From 7 years onwards, the child uses a systematic method; he looks for the smallest of the elements, then the smallest of those which are left over, etc., and in this way easily constructs the series.* This method presupposes the ability to coordinate two inverse relations: $E > D, C,$ B, A and $E < F, G, H$, etc. If we call a the relation expressing the difference between A and B; b the difference between A and C; c the difference between A and D; etc., and a' the difference between B and C; b' the difference between C and D; c' the difference between D and E; etc., we have the following operations:

$$a + a' = b; \quad b + b' = c; \text{ etc.}$$
$$b - a' = a; \quad c - b' = b; \text{ etc.}$$

Other systems appear during the same period having a multiplicative character. For example, the child can classify the same objects taking account of two characteristics at a time, square (A_1) or non-square

* Piaget, *The Child's Conception of Number*, chap. vi.

(A'_1) and red (A_2) and non-red (A'_2). From this we can construct a table of double entry or matrix; the following four cells result from the multiplication:

$$B_1 \times B_2 = A_1 A_2 + A_1 A'_2 + A'_1 A_2 + A'_1 A'_2.$$

In a similar fashion, the child acquires the capacity for multiplying relations using tables of different kinds, correspondences, etc.

These different systems of logical operations are of especial importance in the construction of the concepts of number, time and motion; and in the construction of different geometrical relations (topological, projective and Euclidean).* In this respect, it is of particular interest to analyse how the system of positive and negative integers and the system of linear measure are constructed in close association with the operations of class and relation, but according to methods sometimes differing markedly from those of the logician. For our present purpose, however, details of such a construction are unnecessary.

On the other hand, it is important to emphasize the fact that despite everything acquired in the way of logical techniques during this period of concrete operations, it is, compared with the period which follows, restricted in two essential respects.

The first of these restrictions stems from the insufficiently formal character of the operations at this level. The formal operations are not yet completely dissociated from the concrete data to which they apply. In other words, the operations develop separately field by field, and result in a progressive

* Piaget, *Le Développement de la notion de temps chez l'enfant*, and *Les Notions de mouvement et de vitesse chez l'enfant*, Paris (P.U.F.). Piaget and Inhelder, *La Représentation de l'espace chez l'enfant* (*ibid.*).

structuralization of these fields, without complete generality being attained.

For example, when we show a child two balls of modelling clay of similar dimensions and weight, and shape one of them to look like a sausage or a pancake, three kinds of conservation problems arise: (i) does the altered ball still contain the same quantity of substance as the unaltered one; (ii) does it still have the same weight; (iii) does it still have the same volume, measured by the amount of water it is seen to displace?

The conservation of substance, which in the first period was denied because of the change of perceptual configuration (by the use of such arguments as, 'there is more clay than before, because the thing is longer', and 'there is less because it is thinner', etc.), is from 7 to 8 years onwards felt as a logical necessity and is supported by the following three arguments. (a) The object has only been lengthened (or shortened), and it is easy to restore it to its former shape (simple reversibility); (b) it has been lengthened; but what it has gained in length it has lost in thickness (composition of relations by reversible composition); (c) nothing has been added or taken away (operation of identity which brings us back to the initial state, the product of direct and inverse operations). But these same children deny the conservation of weight for reasons similar to those they used when under 7 to deny the conservation of substance; it is longer, or thinner, etc. Towards 9 to 10 years they admit the conservation of weight, and use by way of proof the same three arguments (a), (b), (c) formulated in exactly the same terms as before! But we find, however, these same children denying at this age the conservation of volume for the very same reasons they formerly used to deny the conservation of substance and weight. Finally, when they are 11 to 12 they once again use the same three arguments to assert the conservation of volume! *

The same results are obtained if we study the conservation of substance, weight and volume with other techniques,† for example, by dissolving a piece of sugar or by soaking popcorn in water. But curiously enough, with respect to all the operations, one finds exactly the same lack of correspondence. For example, children from 7 to 8 onwards are able to order serially objects according to length or size, but it is not until about 9 to 10, on the average, that the serial ordering of objects by weight becomes possible (cf. the seriation of weights in the Binet-Simon tests). From 7 to 8 children become aware of the transitive character of equalities in the case of lengths, etc., but only towards 9 to 10 in the case of weight and towards 11 to 12 for volume.

In short, each field of experience (that of shape and size, weight, etc.) is in turn given a structure by the group of concrete operations, and gives rise in its turn to the construction of invariants (or concepts of conservation). But these operations and invariants cannot be generalized in all fields at once; this leads to a progressive structuring of actual things, but with a time-lag of several years between the different fields or subject-matters. Because of this, concrete operations fail to constitute a formal logic; they are incompletely formalized since form has not yet been completely divorced from subject-matter.

* For a fuller discussion see Piaget and Inhelder, *Le Développement des quantités chez l'enfant* (Delachaux et Niestlé), 1940.
† *Ibid.* chap. iv *et seq.*

Operational systems at this level are restricted in another way—they are fragmentary. We can, with the aid of concrete operations, classify, order serially, form equalities or set up correspondences between objects, etc., without these operations being combined into a single *structured whole*. This fact also prevents concrete operations from constituting a purely formal logic. From the psychological point of view, this means that operations have not yet completely achieved an equilibrium; and this will only occur in the following stage.

(4) *Propositional or formal operations (from 11-12 to 14-15 years).* The final period of operational development begins at about 11 to 12, reaches equilibrium at about 14 to 15 and so leads on to adult logic.

The new feature marking the appearance of this fourth stage is the ability to reason by hypothesis. In verbal thinking such hypothetico-deductive reasoning is characterized, *inter alia*, by the possibility of accepting any sort of data as purely hypothetical, and reasoning correctly from them. For example, when the child has read out to him the following sentences from Ballard's nonsense-sentence test: 'I am very glad I do not eat onions, for if I liked them I would always be eating them and I hate eating unpleasant things', the subject at the concrete level criticizes the data, 'onions are not unpleasant', 'it is wrong not to like them', etc. Subjects at the present level accept the data without discussion, and merely bring out the contradiction between 'if I liked them' and 'onions are unpleasant'.

But it is not only on the verbal plane that the subject reasons by hypothesis. This new capacity has a profound effect on his behaviour in laboratory experiments. Subjects at the propositional level, when shown apparatus of the sort used by my colleague Mlle Inhelder in her investigations into physical inference,* behave quite differently from those at the concrete level. For example, when they are given a pendulum and allowed to vary the length and amplitude of its oscillations, its weights and initial impulse, subjects of 8 to 12 years simply vary the factors in a haphazard way and classify, order serially and set up correspondences between the results obtained. Subjects of 12 to 15 years, on the other hand, endeavour after a few trials to formulate all the possible hypotheses concerning the operative factors, and then arrange their experiments as a function of these factors.

The consequences of this new attitude are as follows. In the first place thought no longer proceeds from the actual to the theoretical, but starts from theory so as to establish or verify actual relationships between things. Instead of just coordinating facts about the actual world, hypothetico-deductive reasoning draws out the implications of possible statements and thus gives rise to a unique synthesis of the possible and necessary.

From this it follows that the subject's logic is now concerned with propositions as well as objects. A group of propositional operations, such as implication $p \supset q$ (if . . . then), disjunction $p \vee q$, incompatibility p/q, etc., is thus constructed. It must be emphasized that it is not simply a case of new linguistic forms expressing, at the level of concrete operations, already

* B. Inhelder, 'Le Raisonnement expérimental chez l'adolescent', *Proceedings and Papers of the Thirteenth Inter. Congress of Psychology at Stockholm* (1951), p. 153.

known relationships between objects. These new operations, particularly those which concern the mechanism of proof, have changed the whole experimental attitude. Mlle Inhelder has, for example, been able to show that the method of difference which varies a single factor at a time, the rest being kept constant, only appears between 12 and 15 years.* It is easy to demonstrate that this method implies propositional operations, since it presupposes a combinatorial system, which arises from something other than the simple setting up of concrete correspondences.

The logic of propositions is especially helpful in that it allows us to discover certain new kinds of invariants, which fall outside the range of empirical verification. For example, in studying the movement of balls of different weights and mass on a horizontal plane, some adolescents are able to state the problem in terms of factors of resistance or rest. If q, r, s, etc., are the statements expressing friction, air resistance, etc., and if p is the statement expressing the fact that the balls have come to rest, their reasoning runs,

$$p \supset (q \lor r \lor s \lor \ldots)$$

from which $(\bar{q} . \bar{r} . \bar{s} . \ldots) \supset \bar{p}$ (its contrapositive).

Hence this deduction (contraposition of the implication) leads them to believe that without the intervention of the factors causing the balls to come to rest (their absence being represented by $(\bar{q} . \bar{r} . \bar{s} . \ldots)$), the movement would continue indefinitely $(\bar{p})$, which is a disguised form of the principle of inertia.

The construction of propositional operations is not the only feature of this fourth period. The most interesting psychological problem raised at this level, is

* B. Ínhelder, *loc. cit.* p. 154.

connected with the appearance of a new group of operations or 'operational schemata', apparently unrelated to the logic of propositions, and whose real nature is not at first apparent.

The first of these operational schemata deals with combinatorial operations in general (combinations, permutations, aggregations). Reference has been made in the introduction to the ability of subjects of 12 years and over to construct all the possible combinations in an experiment based on the random drawing of counters from a bag. Many other examples could be quoted; in particular, the way subjects of 12 to 14 years come to combine in all possible ways n by n five colourless and odourless liquids of different chemical composition, three of which give a coloured product, whilst the fourth removes the colour and the fifth is neutral. While subjects of a lower level mix these liquids at random, the older subjects try them out systematically and keep a strict control over the experiment.

The second operational schema is that of proportions. We have been led to conclude from a large number of different kinds of experiments (dealing with motion, geometrical relations, probabilities as a function of the law of large numbers, proportions between the weights and distances on the two arms of a balance, etc.) that subjects from 8 to 10 are unable to discover the proportionalities involved. From 11 to 12 onwards, on the average, the subject constructs a qualitative schema of proportions which very quickly leads him on to metrical proportions, often without learning about these in school. But why should the understanding of proportions be found at this level and not earlier?

Another operational schema whose construction can be profitably analysed is that of mechanical equilibrium, involving equality between action and reaction. In a system wherein a piston exerts pressure on a liquid contained in two communicating vessels, the subject can only understand the alteration in the level of the liquid by distinguishing four processes, which can most readily be described in terms of operations. (a) The direct operation—i.e. the increase in pressure in the system resulting from the addition of weights to the piston; (b) the inverse operation—i.e. a decrease in pressure resulting from the removal of weights; (c) the reciprocal operation—i.e. the increased resistance of the liquid caused, for example, by an increase in density; (d) the inverse of the reciprocal—i.e. a decrease in the resistance in the liquid. Whereas subjects aged 14 to 15 can easily distinguish these four operations and can correctly coordinate them, young children do not understand that the pressure of the liquid, as shown by its level in the vessel, acts in opposition to the pressure of the piston.

We need only mention the other operational schemata relating to probabilities, correlations, multiplicative compensations, etc. The foregoing examples indicate how they may be translated into logical operations.

This fourth period therefore includes two important acquisitions. Firstly, the logic of propositions, which is both a formal structure holding independently of content and a general structure coordinating the various logical operations into a single system. Secondly, a series of operational schemata which have no apparent connection with each other nor with the logic of propositions.

III

OPERATIONAL STRUCTURES OF THE ALGEBRA OF LOGIC

WE WILL now see whether by using the operational techniques which logic provides we can discover (or construct by their means) structures which can be put into correspondence with the operational structures of psychology.

However, in attempting to compare such mental structures and the structures of modern logic, a difficulty faces us comparable to that which we would find if we tried to compare the intuitive geometry of the child (or of the non-specialist adult) with the axiomatic geometry of Hilbert. Though they are related, we need to introduce intermediate systems and distinguish different levels of formalization in order to make the relationship clear.

As far as formalization is concerned, logic can be conceived from two distinct points of view: (1) logic as an *operational algebra* with its procedures of calculation, its structures, etc.: (2) *axiomatic logic* as the science of truth-conditions, or the theory of formalization itself—this we will call pure or formalized logic.

Axiomatic logic is useless for the particular purpose we have in mind. If we wished to formalize psychological *theories* it would be the only suitable method, but our present aim is to disengage the logical structure of psychological or mental *facts*. We are prevented from using axiomatic or formalized logic for this purpose by three fundamental difficulties.

The first difficulty would be sufficient by itself. It arises from the fact that even the ordinary thinking of the adult is unformalizable. We agree with Bernays that only mathematical thought in its most developed forms permits of a formalization that modern theories of axiomatic logic would recognize as adequate. *A fortiori* the thought of the adult or young child is unformalizable.

The second difficulty is that the order inherent in axiomatization reverses in certain respects the genetic order of the construction of operations. For example, from the axiomatic standpoint the logic of classes is to be deduced from that of propositions, whilst from the genetic point of view propositional operations are derived from the logic of classes and relations. Similarly, for purposes of formalization the axioms precede the algebraic calculus, whilst genetically the axioms are the product of conscious intuition or reflection, directed in the first place by underlying operational mechanisms.

A third difficulty is that axiomatic logic is atomistic in character and the order of its demonstrations necessarily linear. A formalized theory starts from atomic elements (propositions, classes, operations, independent axioms, undefined concepts, etc.), and ends with a closed or completed system built up from these atomic elements. Operational mechanisms, however, have a psychological existence, and are made up of *structured wholes*, the elements of which are connected in the form of a cyclical system irreducible to a linear deduction. In fact, we have here something that resembles more a system involving biological organization than a linear sequence of demonstrations. Thus in our investigation of mental life we must start from the operational structures themselves.

These three difficulties force us to interpolate between psychology and axiomatic logic a *tertium quid*, a 'psycho-logic' or logico-psychology, related to these in the same way as mathematical physics is related to pure mathematics and experimental physics.

Physics is primarily an experimental science concerned exclusively with the study of the material world, and its criterion of truth is agreement with empirical fact. Mathematics, on the other hand, is not based on experiment nor explainable by reference to physical facts; it is a formal science whose sole criterion of truth is the internal consistency appropriate to a rigorous deductive system. The need for explanation in physics itself has led to the application of mathematics to physics and thus given rise to mathematical physics, which has for its object the construction of a deductive theory which will explain the experimental findings.

Without pressing the parallel too far, and without concealing the fact that psychology is some centuries behind physics, we can say that, like physics, it is an experimental science, but one concerned with the study of mental life, whilst its criterion of truth is also agreement with empirical fact. Logic based on the axiomatic method is, on the other hand, a formal science whose sole criterion of truth is deductive rigour.

The need for explanatory schemata in psychology leads us to apply axiomatic logic to psychology itself, and in this way to construct a psycho-logic.* Its task

* Mr. N. Isaacs in his review of my *Traité de logique, Brit. Journ. of Psychol.* (1951), pp. 185-8, has suggested the term 'psycho-logic' to bring out this meaning. This I think to be right, but unfortunately, at the time of writing, I was not sufficiently aware of the need for these three disciplines.

would not, however, be to base logic on psychology, but rather to construct by means of the algebra of logic a deductive theory to explain some of the experimental findings of psychology.*

We will now try to construct logical or algebraic schemata without troubling about the axiomatic requirements of formalized logic, applying simply the two following criteria: (1) these schemata should be logically valid; (2) they should have an adequate application to the findings of experimental psychology.

To construct such schemata we need to start with the most *elementary* structures (not to be confused with the most general), and show by what sort of operations the higher structures are derived from these. We will begin with the first operational structures appearing in the course of the child's intellectual development (period *3*: concrete operations), and try to disengage the corresponding algebraic structures; then go on to propositional structures, returning finally to pre-operational structures.

'Elementary groupements.' The operations of classes and relations at mental level (*3*) correspond to the simple structures which we call 'elementary groupements' and which are definitely limited in scope, if compared to lattices or to the groups characterizing propositional operations or the operations of classes and relations in their most general form (Boolean algebra, etc.).

Simple classification (A included in B, B included in C; etc.) is, for example, based on a system defined by the following five operations:

* See Piaget, 'La Logique axiomatique ou pure, la logique opératoire ou psychologique, et les réalités auxquelles elles correspondent', *Methodos* (Milan), vol. iv (1952), pp. 72-84.

(1) $A + A' = B$; $B + B' = C$; etc. (where $A \times A' = 0$; $B \times B' = 0$; etc.).   [*Composition*]

(2) $-A - A' = -B$; etc., from which $A = B - A'$ and $A' = B - A$.   [*Inversion*]

(3) $A - A = 0$.   [*Identity*]

(4) $A + A = A$ from which $A + B = B$. [*Tautology*]

(5) $A + (A' + B') = (A + A') + B'$ but $A + (A - A) \neq (A + A) - A$.   [*Associativity*]

We see that such compositions of elements into classes can only be carried out *contiguously*, that is to say, by successive inclusions and as a function of the partial complementaries A', B', etc. To take an example:

$$A' + C' = D - A - B'.$$

Similarly, in zoological classification (which conforms to the same schema) the addition of the classes 'sparrows' and 'snails' does not correspond to any elementary class, since they are mutually exclusive. Its only meaning is: 'the class of vertebrates except all classes other than birds and except all birds other than sparrows' + 'the class of invertebrates except all classes other than molluscs and except all molluscs other than snails'.

The structure of this 'elementary groupement' is only a semi-lattice as the *meets* between classes of the same rank are all null: $A \times A' = 0$; $B \times B' = 0$; etc.

Since its associativity is incomplete, it forms an imperfect group, restricted by the tautological operation $A + A = A$.

The *seriation* of asymmetrical transitive relations (or system of serial ordering) exhibits an analogous structure. This may be seen if we express by a, b, c, etc., the differences in their respective order between the first term of the series (A or 0) and each successive term, and by a', b', c', etc., the differences between each term in the series and its immediate successor (i.e. between each pair of terms). Hence, $a+a'=b$; $b+b'=c$, etc., and $b-a'=a$; $a-a=0$; etc.

In a multiplicative groupement, such as the bi-univocal multiplication of classes, the system is defined by the following operations:

(1) $A_1 \times A_2 = A_1 A_2$; $B_1 \times B_2 = A_1 A_2 + A_1 A'_2 + A'_1 A_2 + A'_1 A'_2$; etc.   [*Composition*]

(2) $B_1 B_2 : B_2 = B_1$ (where $:B_2$ means 'eliminating B_2').   [*Inversion*]

(3) $B_1 : B_1 = Z$ (where Z is the most general class of the system obtained by eliminating the inclusion B_1).   [*Identity*]

(4) $B_1 B_2 \times A_1 A_2 = A_1 A_2$.   [*Tautology*]

(5) Associativity restricted by the operations of (4).

Now it is the *join* (between the component classes) which is not general, and once again the complete structure of the lattice is absent.

We can thus construct four groupements of classes and four groupements of relations, which express the totality of operations at the psychological level of concrete operations. We need not refer to them in detail,* but it is useful to point out that these various groupements exhibit two very distinct forms of reversibility.

(a) *Inversion*, which consists in negating a class $(-A)$ or an inclusion $(:A)$. The product of an operation and its inverse is therefore either the null class $(A-A=0)$, or the most general class of the system $(A:A=Z$, since A is a subdivision of Z and if this subdivision is eliminated we arrive back at $Z)$.

---

* See our *Traité de logique*, Paris (Colin).

(b) *Reciprocity*, which consists in eliminating, not a class, or an inclusion (sub-division), but a difference. The product of an operation and its reciprocal gives us not a null class or a universal class but a relation of equivalence: $(A < B) + (A > B) = (A = B)$. We have expressed reciprocity in the language of inversion by formulating it (with respect to seriation) under the form $a - a = 0$.

But if a represents a difference (for example, $A < B$), then o represents the null difference, that is to say, we obtain this equivalence again.

Inversion is the form of reversibility concerned with the operations of classes, and reciprocity the form concerned with the operations of relations. No groupements are present at the level of concrete operations to combine these two kinds of reversibility into a single system. From the standpoint of mental development, inversion (negation or elimination) and reciprocity (symmetry) form two kinds of reversibility, whose beginnings are already to be seen at the lower developmental levels. At the level of concrete operations, they appear in the form of two distinct operational structures (groupements of classes and groupements of relations), and finally form a unique system at the level of propositional operations.

The transition from 'elementary groupements'
of classes and relations to propositional structures

The multiplicative groupement of classes, e.g.

$$A_1 \times A_2 = A_1 A_2; \ B_1 \times B_2 = A_1 A_2 + A_1 A'_2 + A'_1 A_2 + A'_1 A'_2; \ \text{etc.,}$$

arises from the multiplication of two simple classifications. If we make the proposition p correspond to A_1, the proposition q to A_2, the proposition $\bar{p}$ to A'_1 and the proposition $\bar{q}$ to A'_2, the multiplication $B_1 \times B_2$ then corresponds to:

Classes: $(A_1 + A'_1) \times (A_2 + A'_2)$
$$= A_1 A_2 + A_1 A'_2 + A'_1 A_2 + A'_1 A'_2$$
Propositions: $(p \vee \bar{p}) \cdot (q \vee \bar{q})$
$$= (p \cdot q) \vee (p \cdot \bar{q}) \vee (\bar{p} \cdot q) \vee (\bar{p} \cdot \bar{q})$$
Product number 1 2 3 4.

Propositional operations are thus constructed simply by combining n by n these four basic conjunctions. The 16 binary operations of two-valued propositional logic therefore result from the combinations given below (written in numerical form):

0; 1; 2; 3; 4; 12; 13; 14; 23; 24; 34; 123; 124; 134; 234 and 1234.

Elementary groupements are distinguished from the higher groupements which form the system of propositional operations by the fact that the latter is based upon a combinatorial system. Elementary groupements have not yet a complete combinatorial character. For example, multiplicative groupements of classes or relations are solely based on the multiplication of elements 2 by 2 or 3 by 3, etc., but not on combinations among the resultant products (1 to 4 or 1 to 9, etc.), as in the case of the 16 binary propositional operations formed from the products 1 to 4. Another way of expressing the fundamental difference between the two kinds of structures, is to say that elementary groupements are based only on simple sets (the included classes $A < B < C$, etc.) or on product sets (the multiplicative classes A_1A_2; $A_1A'_2$; etc.), whilst propositional structures are based on what is called in the theory of sets a *set of all sub-sets*, combinations taken n by n among the product sets.

We could, of course, easily construct such a combinatorial system, hence a *set of all sub-sets* by means of classes alone. In the case of mental operations at the concrete level, however, such a construction does not take place; which is why combinatorial operations are not included among elementary groupements.

We may therefore ask what operations produce these combinations which make possible the transition of elementary groupements to the *set of all sub-sets*, which is a feature of propositional operations. If we wish to construct algebraic structures which are isomorphic with mental structures, we cannot simply introduce a new operation by the back door. It has to be explained as a function of the preceding operations.

Now the combinatorial system is only a generalization of classification applied to the multiplicative products *1, 2, 3* and *4*. In the classification $A_1+A'_1=B$, we can substitute for the complementary class A'_1 (if A'_1 is not null) a class A_2, and for A_1 the complementary class of A_2, i.e. A'_2, such that (if $<$ represents inclusion)

$$A+A'_1=A_2+A'_2=B \text{ where } A_2<A'_1 \text{ and } A_1<A'_2.$$

This operation, which we call *vicariance*, gives rise to a groupement already present at the level of concrete operations; for example '(the French + the non-French) = (the Chinese + the non-Chinese) = (all men)'. In classifying the products $p . q$; $p . \bar{q}$; $\bar{p} . q$ and $\bar{p} . \bar{q}$ in all possible ways, using the operation of vicariance, we obtain a combinatorial system *n* by *n* and a *set of all sub-sets*.

We can therefore say that the characteristic combinatorial structure of propositional operations forms a groupement of the second order, and consists in applying classification generalized by vicariance to the product sets of the multiplicative groupement. In other words, elementary groupements are groupements of the first order: consisting of (a) simple classifications, (b) vicariances or reciprocal substitutions within the classifications and (c) the multiplication of two or *n* classifications. On the other hand, the combinatorial structure of propositional operations which applies operations (a) and (b) to the products of operation (c), is a groupement of the second order; and hence of a more general form and corresponds to later mental structures.

Propositional structures

In contrast to elementary groupements, which have the structure of semi-lattices and imperfect groups, the *set of all sub-sets* upon which propositional operations are based has the dual structure of a (complete) lattice and a group. The lattice and group structures are combined into a single system which obeys the laws of groupements, since it is a groupement of the second order, without the restrictions noted above (contiguity, etc.).

It is unnecessary to stress the fact that this structure forms a lattice whose *join* is $(p \vee q)$ and whose *meet* is $(p \cdot q)$.

As against this, the 'group' aspect of the structure of propositional operations is generally neglected.

Now this structure is subject to the laws of a group of four transformations (*Vierer-gruppe*), which, from the point of view of operational mechanisms, is of great importance.

An operation such as $(p \vee q)$ has an *inverse N* distinct from it, namely $(\bar{p} \cdot \bar{q})$ and which in relation to the set $(p \cdot q) \vee (p \cdot \bar{q}) \vee (\bar{p} \cdot q) \vee (\bar{p} \cdot \bar{q})$ is its complementary. It also has a reciprocal R (distinct or not), which is the same operation between negated propositions. In the case of $p \vee q$, the reciprocal R is distinct, and is $\bar{p} \vee \bar{q}$, that is to say, p/q. Finally, it has a correlate C (distinct or not) resulting from the permutation of $(\vee)$ and of $(.)$ in the corresponding normal form: the correlate in this case is $(p \cdot q)$. On adding the identity transformation (I) to these three transformations they form a commutative group:

(1) $CR = N$; $RN = C$; $NC = R$; and (2) $NRC = I$.

Other examples are: if $I = (p \supset q)$, then $N = (p \cdot \bar{q})$, $R = (q \supset p)$, $C = (\bar{p} \cdot q)$.

If $I = (p = q)$, then $N = (p \text{ w } q)$, $R = (\bar{p} = \bar{q}) = (p = q)$, $C = (\bar{p} \text{ w } \bar{q}) = (p \text{ w } q)$; etc.
(where w symbolizes the reciprocal exclusion $p = \bar{q}$ and $\bar{p} = q$).

Thus the two forms of reversibility, inversion (N) and reciprocity (R), are found combined in a single system, while they remain separate in the field of elementary groupements.

To bring out the close connection between the lattice and group aspects of propositional operations, we can arrange these operations in the form of a single table. The elements of this table (numbered from the top horizontally starting from the left) are formed from four unary operations.

D

$$q \cdot \bar{q} \ (=0); \ q \ ; \ \bar{q} \ ; \ q \vee \bar{q}$$

multiplied by p or by $\bar{q}$:

$1 \ (0)$	$2 \ (p \cdot q)$	$3 \ (p \cdot \bar{q})$	$4 \ p \cdot (q \vee \bar{q})$
$5 \ (\bar{p} \cdot \bar{q})$	$8 \ (p \cdot q) \vee (\bar{p} \cdot \bar{q})$	$11 \ (p \cdot \bar{q}) \vee (\bar{p} \cdot \bar{q})$	$14 \ (q \supset p)$
$6 \ (\bar{p} \cdot q)$	$9 \ (p \cdot q) \vee (\bar{p} \cdot q)$	$12 \ (p \cdot \bar{q}) \vee (\bar{p} \cdot q)$	$15 \ (p \vee q)$
$7 \ \bar{p} \cdot (q \vee \bar{q})$	$10 \ (p \supset q)$	$13 \ (p/q)$	$16 \ (p \cdot q) \vee (p \cdot \bar{q})$
			$(p \cdot q) \vee (\bar{p} \cdot \bar{q})$

We observe that:

(1) Elements 8 to 16 are each the logical sum (v) of the element at the top of the same column, and the element at the extreme left of the same row. For example: $8 \ (p=q) = 2 \ (p \cdot q) \vee 5 \ (\bar{p} \cdot \bar{q})$.

(2) Elements 1 to 3; 5, 8 and 11; 6, 9 and 12 are the logical product (.) of the element at the extreme right of the same row and the element at the foot of the same column. For example: $8 \ (p=q) = 14 \ (q \supset p) \cdot 10 \ (p \supset q)$.

(3) Each element has for its inverse N its symmetrical in relation to the centre of the table: for example $2 \ (p \cdot q)$ and $13 \ (p/q)$, or $14 \ (q \supset p)$ and $6 \ (\bar{p} \cdot q)$.

(4) Each element has for its reciprocal R its symmetrical in relation to the diagonal ⬊ : for example, $14 \ (q \supset p)$ and $10 \ (p \supset q)$.

(5) Each element has for its correlate C its symmetrical in relation to the diagonal ⬈ : for example, $2 \ (p \cdot q)$ and $15 \ (p \vee q)$.

(6) The elements of the diagonal ⬊ (therefore 1, 8, 12 and 16) exhibit the properties $I=R$ and $C=N$. For example, the R of 8 is 8 and the N of 8 is 12 which is also its C.

(7) The elements of the diagonal ⬈ (therefore 7, 9, 11 and 4) exhibit the properties $I=C$ and

$R=N$. For example, the N of 9 is 11, which is also its R and the C of 9 is 9.

We can construct a similar table, with the same seven properties (and several others besides) by means of the 256 tertiary operations, the $65,536$ quaternary operations, etc.*

Now from the group $INRC$, we can deduce a system of *logical proportions* (restricting ourselves to the group transformations and without introducing the tautological operations $p \cdot p = p$ or $p \vee p = p$).

We shall say that the four operations α, β, γ and δ are proportionals if we have:

$$\frac{\alpha}{\beta}=\frac{\gamma}{\delta} \quad \text{if (1)} \quad \alpha \cdot \delta = \beta \cdot \gamma \quad \text{and (2)} \quad \alpha \vee \delta = \beta \vee \gamma$$

and if in these two equations we can transpose from one side to the other by transforming $(\vee x)$ into $(. \, \bar{x})$ or $(. \, x)$ into $(\vee \bar{x})$.

From which we get the properties (3-6) deduced from (2) and (7-10) deduced from (1):

(3) $\alpha \cdot \bar{\beta} = \gamma \cdot \bar{\delta}$ (5) $\bar{\alpha} \cdot \beta = \bar{\gamma} \cdot \delta$ (7) $\alpha \vee \bar{\beta} = \gamma \vee \bar{\delta}$ (9) $\bar{\alpha} \vee \beta = \bar{\gamma} \vee \delta$

(4) $\alpha \cdot \bar{\gamma} = \beta \cdot \bar{\delta}$ (6) $\bar{\alpha} \cdot \gamma = \bar{\beta} \cdot \delta$ (8) $\alpha \vee \bar{\gamma} = \beta \vee \bar{\delta}$ (10) $\bar{\alpha} \vee \gamma = \bar{\beta} \vee \delta$.

We then observe that four operations are to be found in the relationships I, N, R and C which always satisfy these conditions:†

$$\frac{I}{R}=\frac{C}{N}, \text{ for example } \frac{p \vee q}{p/q}=\frac{p \cdot q}{\bar{p} \cdot \bar{q}}$$

* See our book, *Essai sur les transformations des opérations logiques. Les 256 opérations ternaires de la logique bivalente*, Paris, 1952 (P.U.F.).

† Translator's note: To take two examples:

(1) $[\alpha \cdot \delta = \beta \cdot \gamma]$ $I \cdot N = R \cdot C$. E.g. $(p \vee q) \cdot (\bar{p} \cdot \bar{q}) = (p/q) \cdot (p \cdot q)$.

(3) $[\alpha \cdot \bar{\beta} = \gamma \cdot \bar{\delta}]$ $I \cdot \bar{R} = C \cdot \bar{N}$. E.g. $(p \vee q) \cdot \overline{(p/q)} = (p \cdot q) \cdot (\overline{\bar{p} \cdot \bar{q}})$.

since: (1) $(p \vee q) \cdot (\bar{p} \cdot \bar{q}) = (p / q) \cdot (\underline{p} \cdot q) = 0$
           (3) $(p \vee q) \cdot (\overline{p / q}) = (p \cdot q) \cdot (\bar{p} \cdot \bar{q}) = (p \cdot q)$
           etc.

Proportionality may be extended to elements between which the relationships I, N, R, C do not hold, subject to the condition that the group transformations apply. We can, for example, add $(\vee x)$ to α if we add $(.\bar{x})$ to δ, but only if x has no common part with α. Similarly, $(\vee x)$ may be eliminated in α, if $(.\bar{x})$ is eliminated in δ, provided that x is wholly part of α.

From $\dfrac{p \vee q}{p \cdot q} = \dfrac{\bar{p} \vee \bar{q}}{\bar{p} \cdot \bar{q}}$ we can therefore deduce $\dfrac{p}{q} = \dfrac{\bar{q}}{\bar{p}}$ by eliminating $(\vee q)$ in α and $(.\bar{q})$ in δ, and by eliminating $(\vee \bar{p})$ in γ and $(.p)$ in β.

In the same way a system of reciprocal proportions may be deduced from the preceding conditions,

$$\frac{\alpha}{\beta} = R\frac{\gamma}{\delta} \quad \text{if} \quad \begin{array}{ll} (1) & \alpha \cdot \delta = R(\beta \cdot \gamma) \\ (2) & \alpha \vee \delta = R(\beta \vee \gamma) \end{array} \quad \begin{array}{l} (3) \;\; \alpha \cdot C\beta = R(\gamma \cdot C\delta) \\ \qquad\quad \text{etc.} \end{array}$$

For example $\dfrac{p}{q} = R\dfrac{\bar{p}}{\bar{q}}$ since $p \cdot \bar{q} = R(\bar{p} \cdot q)$ and $p \cdot q = R(\bar{p} \cdot \bar{q})$; etc.

It should be noted that these unary proportions correspond to numerical proportions:

$$\frac{p}{q} = \frac{\bar{q}}{\bar{p}} \text{ corresponds to } \frac{nx}{ny} = \frac{n{:}y}{n{:}x} \text{ and } \frac{p}{q} = R\frac{\bar{p}}{\bar{q}} \text{ corresponds}$$

to
$$\frac{nx}{ny} = \frac{x{:}n}{y{:}n}.$$

Finally, we should note that from the proportion $\dfrac{I}{C} = \dfrac{R}{N}$ with the help of the preceding transformations and the deductions therefrom, we easily arrive at the following well-known proportion of lattice theory:

$$\frac{x \cdot y}{x} = \frac{y}{x \vee y} \quad \text{for example,} \quad \frac{p \cdot q}{p} = \frac{q}{p \vee q}.$$

The above proportion exhibits the same properties as the proportion $\dfrac{I}{C} = \dfrac{R}{N}$, but is naturally subject to the condition of asserting,

$$p = (p \cdot q) \vee (p \cdot \bar{q}) \quad \text{and} \quad q = (p \cdot q) \vee (\bar{p} \cdot q).$$

It would be easy to specify many other properties of this combined group and lattice structure, especially in the case of the 256 ternary operations, which contain numerous other kinds of transformations. But for the purpose of explaining the mental operations described under § II, the above account is adequate.

Translator's Notes

(1) *Logical Groupements.* Unlike a mathematical group (cf. pp. xiv-xv), a logical groupement is defined by five operations (cf. principles 1-5, pp. 27-8) and includes the restrictive condition of tautology (principle 4). In arithmetic a unit added to itself gives a new number $1 + 1 = 2$, but repeating a logical element only gives a tautology $A + A = A$.

(2) *The table of 16 propositional operations (p. 34).* This is isomorphic with a truth-value table for two propositions, in which all the possible products are listed. The relationships between the elements of the above table (the set of transformations $INRC$) form a commutative group.

(3) *Logical proportions.* This resembles Spearman's principle of the 'eduction of correlates' (cf. Piaget, *Classes, Relations et Nombres*, pp. 97-9 (Vrin, 1942)). We proceed by establishing a relationship between two pairs of terms on the model of an arithmetical ratio (e.g. $\frac{2}{4} = \frac{3}{6}$), such that the relation existing between the first pair recurs in the case of the second pair and thus determines the choice of the fourth term.

IV

CONCLUSION: THE PSYCHOLOGICAL MEANING OF THESE LOGICAL STRUCTURES

WE HAVE described under § II the operational structures from a psychological point of view, and analysed under § III a certain number of structures in terms of the algebra of logic, but we still have to bring out the correspondence between these two systems, and explain how algebraic structures can be used in psychological explanation. For this purpose it will be convenient to deal with the higher structures first, and then come back to the simpler ones.

Propositional structures

To give a complete account of these structures we would have to show that the *16* binary operations of two-valued propositional logic are present in the intuitive thought of adolescents aged 12 to 15. But it is unnecessary to give examples here, as we have already shown that adolescents do, in fact, use these *16* binary operations, as well as a certain number of ternary operations or operations of a higher rank.

Further, and this is extremely important, the subject can proceed from any one of these operations to any other. On the other hand, the child aged 7 to 11 when given an inductive problem in physics, as in the case of Mlle Inhelder's problems, limits himself to the raw experimental data. He classifies, orders the data in series, sets up correspondences between them, etc., but does not isolate the factors involved or embark upon systematic experimentation. The adolescent, however, after several preliminary attempts tries to discover all possible combinations, so as to select the true and discard the false. In the course of this selective activity he intuitively constructs a combinatorial system. It is for this reason that he repeatedly passes from one propositional operation to another. The method of solution in each actual problem situation then consists in the selection of the true combination (or combinations) out of the whole set of possible combinations.

Propositional operations do not therefore appear in the adolescent's thought as unrelated discrete operations; they form a system or *structured whole*. What we have to discover is in what manner this structure is given for the subject.

As we have seen, the fact that the logic of propositions proceeds from the possible (i.e. theoretical) to the actual and consists in truth-selections, leads to a very simple hypothesis as to the psychological meaning of the system of propositional operations; and consequently, as to the way in which the *structured wholes*, such as the lattice or the group *INRC*, which are a feature of these operations, appear in the child's mind.

If this hypothesis were not accepted, what other explanation could we give for these structures? By way of a first hypothesis they might be regarded as the cumulative product of past experience. But such an interpretation seems improbable since they are completely unconscious. The adolescent is not conscious of the system of propositional operations.

He undoubtedly uses these operations, but he does this without enumerating them, or reflecting on them or their relationships, and he only faintly suspects that they form such a system. He is unaware of this, in the same way that in singing or whistling he is unaware of the laws of harmony. The view that such unconscious structures result from a summation of acquired experiences is thus quite unacceptable.

A second hypothesis would be to treat these structures as *a priori* forms of the mind; for such forms, if they exist, can remain unconscious and nevertheless still influence the development of thought. But if we really are concerned here with *a priori* forms why do they appear at so late a stage?

A third hypothesis might be to regard them as arising from the late maturation of certain neural connections (we know, for example, that it is possible to apply propositional operations to neural networks).* But if the logical *structured wholes* exist as ready-made traces in the nervous system, they ought to appear in their entirety during thinking. This is simply not the case: only certain parts of such structures are actualized, the rest remain in the form of possible transformations.

We thus come to our fourth and last hypothesis, already touched upon, in which the lattice and the group *INRC* are regarded as structures belonging to the simple forms of equilibrium attained by thought activity. In the first place these structures appear psychologically in the form of a few concrete operations, but what is more important they provide a field of possible transformations.

* W. S. McCulloch and W. Pitts, *Bull. math. Biophys.*, vol. 5 (1943), pp. 115-33.

A state of equilibrium, it should be remembered, is one in which all the virtual transformations compatible with the relationships of the system compensate each other. From a psychological point of view, the logical structures correspond precisely to this model. On the one hand, these structures appear in the form of a set of virtual transformations, consisting of all the operations which it would be possible to carry out starting from a few actually performed operations. On the other, these structures are essentially reversible, that is to say, the virtual transformations which they permit are always self-compensatory as a consequence of inversions and reciprocities.

In this way, we can explain why the subject is affected by such structures, without being conscious of them. When starting from an actually performed propositional operation, or endeavouring to express the characters of a given situation by such an operation, he cannot proceed in any way he likes. He finds himself, as it were, in a field of force governed by the laws of equilibrium, carrying out transformations or operations determined not only by occurrences in the immediate past, but by the laws of the whole operational field of which these past occurrences form a part.

We can now understand the paradox resulting from the simultaneous appearance of operational schemata (such as combinations, proportions, the schema of mechanical equilibrium) and of propositional operations, whose connection remains unperceived by the subject, and whose kinship the psychologist is unable to appreciate in his ignorance of algebraic structures. Operational schemata are thus to be thought of as actualized structures, implying the diverse possibilities implicit in the *structured whole*, that is to say, in the form of equilibrium of the propositional operations.

Mathematical combinatorial operations are formed systematically from the first, whenever the situation or problem demands it; since the subject, when he coordinates experiential data and especially when he selects out of all the possible propositional operations those which fit this particular arrangement of data, is concerned with an implicit combinatorial system. This combinatorial system implied by the lattice of propositional operations is therefore derived by abstraction from the operational constructions intuitively arrived at by the subject. Hence, it is not due to chance that this system appears at the same level of intellectual development as the logic of propositions.

The concept of mechanical equilibrium, too, is only understood at the same period except of course, when all the given data are simultaneously visible in an intuitively simple system. We have seen under § II that subjects have difficulty in distinguishing four transformations: increase or decrease of action and increase or decrease of reaction. The reaction (for example, the resistance of a liquid to the pressure of a piston) is not understood by small children as occurring in an inverse sense to that of action (resistance), but as a force which adds itself to the latter (the heavier the liquid the higher it can rise). To be able to solve this problem, the child has to coordinate the inversions (increase and decrease of action or reaction) and reciprocities. In fact, the reaction conceived as equal to the action but occurring in an inverse sense is a typical example of the relation of reciprocity. It is then natural to assume that the capacity for coordinating these inversions and reciprocities into a single system is based on an understanding of the logical relationships of inversion (CN) and reciprocity (R); therefore of the group $INRC$. Reciprocity can, in fact, have the same resultant as inversion, without necessarily becoming confused with it; similarly, the inversion of reciprocity (C) can without confusion have the same resultant as the identity transformation (I). The above assumption has a good deal to support it as subjects at this level (12 to 15 years) after having failed at the lower levels, are able to coordinate the four transformations $INRC$ in quite different problems; such as those of relative motion, i.e. the prediction of changes in position of a moving body within a framework of reference itself in motion in relation to a fixed system (for example, the changes in position of a snail on a moving board).* All this seems to occur as if the acquisition of the logic of propositions went together with an understanding of the group $INRC$, not, of course, *in abstracto*, but as applied to various problems.

An important application of this 'group' logic occurs, as we have seen, in the scheme of logical proportionality. It is striking once again to observe that this schema appears at the level of development at which the child begins to understand mathematical proportions. No doubt it will be objected that, since mathematical proportions are equalities between two relationships, they are much simpler than propositional proportions and can be constructed independently of them. But the following two facts need noting. In the first place, if the child had directly understood the mathematical concept without the aid of the system of propositional operations, there would be no

---

* See Piaget, *Les Notions de mouvement et de vitesse chez l'enfant*, Paris (P.U.F.).

reason why this mathematical concept should not already be implicit in his thinking at the level of concrete operations, since the concept of a fraction is derivative from that of inclusion, and the equality of two fractions merely presents an additional difficulty of a trivial kind.

But, in all the fields we have examined, the schema of proportionality is only understood at the level of propositional operations. Further, all these systems of proportions which the child discovers for himself without schooling are found by means of a logical qualitative schema. The child begins by noting certain compensations or equivalences; for example, the weight on a balance may be increased whilst its distance from the fulcrum remains unchanged, or the distance may be increased and the weight left constant. He then coordinates the inversions and reciprocities, and thus arrives at a qualitative statement of the proportion which he verifies by measuring, and in this way finally discovers the metrical proportion.

What therefore has to be explained is this anticipatory qualitative schema, which is why we believe that, psychologically, proportionality begins through the logical schema $\frac{p}{q}=\frac{\bar{q}}{\bar{p}}$ or $\frac{p}{q}=R\frac{\bar{p}}{\bar{q}}$, which in turn is based on the group $INRC$.

The above interpretation is made more plausible by the fact that, in many fields, the subject aged 12 to 14, without recourse to measurement or other quantitative methods, arrives at a qualitative schema—that of 'multiplicative compensations'—which is closely akin to that of proportions. For example, in the case of changes in the form of an object it may be asked why the conservation of volume is only acquired in a general form towards the age of 12? The reason for this is that an increase in one of the dimensions is compensated by a corresponding decrease in the two others, in accordance with a multiplicative system implying proportionality. Once again, reasoning is shown to be dependent on an anticipatory schema, whose connection with the preceding schemata is fairly evident.

Other examples might be given, such as the combinatorial probabilities (assuming that it is through such combinations that possibility and fact are brought together), correlations (based on the quantification of the four conjunctions $p \cdot q$; $p \cdot \bar{q}$; $\bar{p} \cdot q$ and $\bar{p} \cdot \bar{q}$), etc. But we do not need to enter into details here.

What we have already said justifies the following conclusion: the construction of propositional operations is accompanied by a series of changes in the subject's capacity to perform operations. The different schemata which he acquires are shown to imply not merely isolated propositional operations, but the *structured wholes* themselves (the lattice and the group *INRC*) which the propositional operations exemplify. The *structured whole*, considered as the form of equilibrium of the subject's operational behaviour, is therefore of fundamental psychological importance, which is why the logical (algebraic) analysis of such structures gives the psychologist an indispensable instrument of explanation and prediction.

*Concrete operational structures and
pre-operational structures*

The use of the algebra of logic is not, however, restricted to an analysis of psychological activities at the level of propositional operations. The eight groupements of classes and relations, constructed at the level of concrete operations, are of equal value in the study of behaviour at this earlier level. The psychological problem at this stage is to construct a catalogue of possible operations for a mode of thought to which the combinatorial system implied by the lattice structure is still alien; and to explain why this mode of thought is unable to achieve a general formal mechanism independently of its content. The system of eight groupements answers these two questions. In the first place, it gives an exhaustive catalogue of concrete operations, since their number is not arbitrary, but is made up as follows: classes and relations (*2*), addition and multiplication (*2*), symmetry and asymmetry (*2*), hence $2 \times 2 \times 2 = 8$. Secondly, we have here eight interdependent systems, and not a single system enabling us to pass from one operation to any other, and this explains the absence of a general formal mechanism.

At the concrete level (7 to 11 years), elementary groupements, such as the group and lattice structure of propositional operations, make up the form of equilibrium of operational behaviour, but an equilibrium less stable and covering a less extended field. We thus have to find out how this equilibrium comes about. Though we know that the final equilibrium is prepared and partly organized at the pre-operational level (2 to 7 years), we still have to show what mechanisms at this pre-operational level are the precursors of the future operations.

I term these mechanisms 'regulations'. They are to be conceived of as partial compensations or partial returns to the starting-point, with compensatory adjustments accompanying changes in the direction of the original activity. Such regulations are found in the sensori-motor field (perceptions, etc.), and they come more and more to govern the representations preceding the operational level. For example, when we stretch a sausage-shaped piece of modelling clay, the child assumes there has been an increase in the amount of the material. Finally when it becomes very thin he gets the impression that the amount of material has diminished.

Such regulations which apply to the fields of perception and representation can also be formulated in terms of the algebra of logic. All we need to do is to express the transformations in terms of groupements, and transform the resultant logical inequalities into equalities, by adding the 'non-compensated transformations' $+P$ or $-P$ as the case may be.

The particular advantage of this kind of formulation is that it brings out the difference between the changes (irreversible or not wholly reversible) occurring in perception or representation, and the corresponding reversible transformations which characterize operations. We have, for example, made use of this method in the analysis of perceptions, in spite of the absence of additive composition and logical coherence which is a feature of this mode of experience. The concrete operations which belong to the 7 to 8 level can then be considered as the resultant of these regulations when they reach a state of equilibrium, the point where equilibrium is reached being that of complete compensation. In other words, at the point where complete reversibility is achieved, 'regulations of representations' are *ipso facto* transformed into operations. This is therefore the final form of equilibrium of regulations, and bears some resemblance to the way in which *feed-back* (regulation) operates in a servo-mechanism as long as there is disequilibrium, and as soon as equilibrium is reached, takes on the form of a group.

Thus, even in those fields in which logic does not normally play a part, there exist *outline structures* which are the precursors of logical structures, and which can be formulated in terms of the algebra of logic. From a comparative point of view, these *outline structures* are of great interest. It is not inconceivable that a general theory of structures will at some future date be worked out, which will permit the comparative analysis of structures characterizing the different levels of development. This will relate the lower level *outline structures* to the logical structures characteristic of the higher stages of development. The use of the logical calculus in the description of neural networks on the one hand, and in cybernetic models on the other, shows that such a programme is not out of the question.

Though the preceding discussion is concerned only with certain levels of the intellectual development of the child and adolescent, I should be glad if it could be regarded as a contribution to such studies.